W9-AZS-207

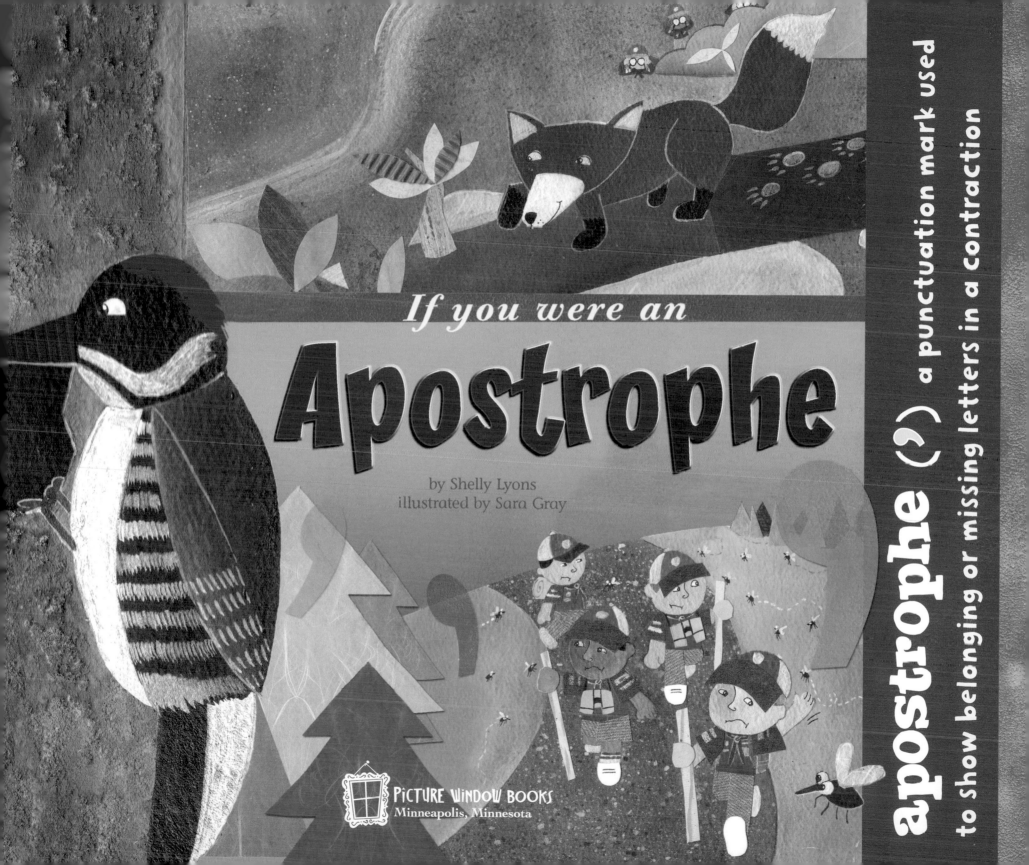

If you were an

Apostrophe

by Shelly Lyons

illustrated by Sara Gray

PICTURE WINDOW BOOKS
Minneapolis, Minnesota

apostrophe (') a punctuation mark used to show belonging or missing letters in a contraction

For Sean and Eliot, two boys who have opened up my eyes

Editor: Jill Kalz
Designer: Tracy Davies
Page Production: Melissa Kes
Art Director: Nathan Gassman
Editorial Director: Nick Healy
The illustrations in this book were created with acrylics.

Picture Window Books
151 Good Counsel Drive
P.O. Box 669
Mankato, MN 56002-0669
877-845-8392
www.picturewindowbooks.com

Printed in the United States of America.

All books published by Picture Window Books are
manufactured with paper containing at least
10 percent post-consumer waste.

Library of Congress Cataloging-in-Publication Data
Lyons, Shelly.
If you were an apostrophe / by Shelly Lyons ;
illustrated by Sara Gray.
p. cm. — (Word Fun)
Includes index.
ISBN 978-1-4048-5317-1 (library binding)
ISBN 978-1-4048-5318-8 (paperback)
1. English language—Punctuation—Juvenile literature.
2. Apostrophe—Juvenile literature. 3. Language arts
(Primary) I. Gray, Sara. II. Title.
PE1450.L93 2009
428.2—dc22
2008039324

Special thanks to our advisers
for their expertise:

Rosemary G. Palmer, Ph.D.
Department of Literacy
College of Education
Boise State University

Terry Flaherty, Ph.D.
Professor of English
Minnesota State University, Mankato

Looking for apostrophes?

Watch for the BIG marks throughout the book.

If you were
an apostrophe ...

Lake
Superior

N
W E
S

3

... you could be

the **park's** picnic table,

Chad's tent,

4

or the **scouts'** campfire.

If you were an apostrophe, you would show belonging.
You would show that something belongs to a noun.
A noun is a word that names a person, place, or thing.

A **mosquito's** buzzing
bothers a scout on the
park's woody trail.

The **boy**'s loud SWAT scares the mosquito away.

If you were an apostrophe, you could show that something belongs to more than one person, place, or thing.

The **wolves'** teeth glow white in the moonlight.

8

The **owls'** hoots echo throughout the park.

A racoon steals the **scouts'** bag of treats.

If you were an apostrophe, you would appear in a contraction. A contraction is a word made by joining two words and leaving out a letter or letters. If you were an apostrophe, you would take the place of the missing letter or letters.

A moose **does not** mind swimming. It **doesn't** mind swimming on a sunny afternoon.

In fact, **it will** dip and dive.
It'll make a big splash.

If you were an apostrophe, you would shorten a sentence.

The loon **would have** enjoyed singing to a quiet crowd.

The loon **would've** enjoyed singing to a quiet crowd.

13

If you were an apostrophe, you might make a contraction incorrectly. You might try to sit between the two words.

Incorrect: The sunfish **should'nt** jump and splash so loudly.

If you were an apostrophe, you would belong where letters are missing.

Correct: The sunfish **shouldn't** jump and splash so loudly.

If you were an apostrophe, you would not show belonging for the pronoun *it*. *Its* shows belonging. *It's* is a contraction of "it is" or "it has."

A red fox uses **its** long, bushy tail to keep **its** balance.

It's the long, bushy tail that helps the fox stay balanced.

16

If you were an apostrophe, you would make single letters plural.

Two herons form **m's** as they lift their wings.

Three lake trout make **s's** as they swish away.

Four **ð's** peek through the forest brush.

If you were an apostrophe, you would help tell time. *O'clock is short for "of the clock."*

At 6 **o'clock**, a woodpecker hammers against a tree.

At 1 **o'clock**, a duck floats atop the waves.

At 8 **o'clock**, two deer gaze at the campfire.

You'd be busy on the lakeshore showing belonging,
standing in for letters, and telling time ...

... if you were an apostrophe.

Quick Review

An apostrophe shows belonging.

The boy's mother put sunscreen on him.
The loons' songs made us smile.

Its shows belonging. *It's* is short for "it is" or "it has."

A long tail helps the fox keep its (shows belonging) balance.
It's (it is) the tail that helps the fox stay balanced.

An apostrophe takes the place of the missing letter or letters in a contraction.

How'd (how did) that moose swim so quickly?

Apostrophes make single letters plural.

Garter snakes form s's as they slither.

Apostrophes help tell time.

The sun sets at 9 o'clock.

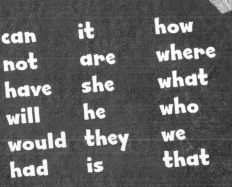

Fun with Apostrophes

Gather a group of friends. Each person should have a piece of paper and a pen or pencil. Set a timer for one minute. Using the words to the right, write down as many contractions as you can. Be sure to use apostrophes correctly.

When you're done, have an adult check your work. The person who forms the most contractions and correctly uses apostrophes wins!

can	it	how
not	are	where
have	she	what
will	he	who
would	they	we
had	is	that

Glossary

apostrophe—a punctuation mark used to show belonging or missing letters in a contraction

contraction—a word made by combining two words and leaving out a letter or letters

noun—a word that names a person, place, or thing

plural—more than one

pronoun—a word that takes the place of a noun

punctuation—marks that make written language clear

single—just one

To Learn More

More Books to Read

Carr, Jan. *Greedy Apostrophe: A Cautionary Tale.* New York: Holiday House, 2007.

Donohue, Moira Rose. *Alfie the Apostrophe.* Morton Grove, Ill.: Albert Whitman & Co., 2006.

Pulver, Robin. *Punctuation Takes a Vacation.* New York: Holiday House, 2003.

Salzmann, Mary Elizabeth. *Apostrophe.* Edina, Minn.: ABDO Pub., 2001.

On the Web

FactHound offers a safe, fun way to find educator-approved Internet sites related to this book.

Here's what you do:
1. Visit *www.facthound.com*
2. Choose your grade level.
3. Begin your search.

This book's ID number is 9781404853171

Look for all of the books in the Word Fun: Punctuation series:

If You Were a Comma
If You Were a Period
If You Were a Question Mark
If You Were an Apostrophe
If You Were an Exclamation Point
If You Were Quotation Marks